HUMAN DARK
WITH SUGAR

HUMAN DARK WITH SUGAR

BRENDA SHAUGHNESSY

COPPER CANYON PRESS

PORT TOWNSEND, WASHINGTON

Printed in the United States of America

Cover art: Judith Linhares, *Plenty*, 2002. Oil on linen, 58 x 78 inches. Courtesy of Edward Thorp Gallery, New York.

Copper Canyon Press is in residence at Fort Worden State Park in Port Townsend, Washington, under the auspices of Centrum. Centrum is a gathering place for artists and creative thinkers from around the world, students of all ages and backgrounds, and audiences seeking extraordinary cultural enrichment.

LIBRARY OF CONGRESS CATALOGING-IN-PUBLICATION DATA
Shaughnessy, Brenda, 1970–
  Human dark with sugar / Brenda Shaughnessy.
    p. cm.
  ISBN 978-1-55659-276-8 (pbk. : alk. paper)
  I. Title.
  PS3569.H353H86 2008
  811'.54—dc22

                                        2007052225

98765432 FIRST PRINTING

COPPER CANYON PRESS
Post Office Box 271
Port Townsend, Washington 98368
www.coppercanyonpress.org

ACKNOWLEDGMENTS

I'd like to thank the editors of the following publications in which these poems appeared, sometimes in slightly different versions.

Bomb: "I'm Over the Moon," "Three Summers Mark Only Two Years," "Straight's the New Gay"

Born.com: "Fathometer"

Boston Review: "Sorry, T."

The Canary: "One Love Story, Eight Takes"

Colorado Review: "This Loved Body"

Columbia Poetry Review: "A Poet's Poem," "Moth Death on the Windowsill," "A Brown Age"

Conjunctions: "Breasted Landscape"

Gulf Coast: "First Date and Still Very, Very Lonely," "Dancing Alone in my Room"

Isn't It Romantic: 100 Love Poems by Younger American Poets: "Me in Paradise"

jubilat: "Drift," "Three Sorries"

McSweeney's: "I'm Over the Moon," "Why Is the Color of Snow?"

Nerve.com: "I'm Perfect at Feelings," "Me in Paradise"

The New Yorker: "Magician"

The Paris Review: "Embarrassment"

Quarterly West: "Parthenogenesis," "Magic Turns to Math and Back"

Radcliffe Quarterly: "Spring in Space: A Lecture"

I wish to thank the Radcliffe Institute for Advanced Study, the Japan-U.S. Friendship Commission, and the Corporation of Yaddo for their generous and varied gifts of time, funds, and travel. I am especially grateful to everyone connected with the amazing MacDowell colony, where much of this book was inspired and written.

I am very grateful to my family and friends, colleagues, employers, and students. In particular, I wish to thank my sister Lisa, my friends at *Tin House*, The Academy of American Poets, and Michael Wiegers at Copper Canyon Press. I will always be grateful to Bill Wadsworth, Dorothea Tanning, and Richard Howard for their friendship and kindness.

This book is dedicated to my two great loves: my husband, Craig, and my son, Calvin.

CONTENTS

ASTROLABE

HUMAN DARK
WITH SUGAR

ANODYNE

I'm Over the Moon

I don't like what the moon is supposed to do.
Confuse me, ovulate me,

spoon-feed me longing. A kind of ancient
date-rape drug. So I'll howl at you, moon,

I'm angry. I'll take back the night. Using me to
swoon at your questionable light,

you had me chasing you,
the world's worst lover, over and over

hoping for a mirror, a whisper, insight.
But you disappear for nights on end

with all my erotic mysteries
and my entire unconscious mind.

How long do I try to get water from a stone?
It's like having a bad boyfriend in a good band.

Better off alone. I'm going to write hard
and fast into you, moon, face-fucking.

Something you wouldn't understand.
You with no swampy sexual

promise but what we glue onto you.
That's not real. You have no begging

cunt. No panties ripped off and the crotch
sucked. No lacerating spasms

sending electrical sparks through the toes.
Stars have those.

What do you have? You're a tool, moon.
Now, noon. There's a hero.

The obvious sun, no bullshit, the enemy
of poets and lovers, sleepers and creatures.

But my lovers have never been able to read
my mind. I've had to learn to be direct.

It's hard to learn that, hard to do.
The sun is worth ten of you.

You don't hold a candle
to that complexity, that solid craze.

Like an animal carcass on the road at night,
picked at by crows,

haunting walkers and drivers. Your face
regularly sliced up by the moving

frames of car windows. Your light is drawn,
quartered, your dreams are stolen.

You change shape and turn away,
letting night solve all night's problems alone.

Magic Turns to Math and Back

If time were tellable, we wouldn't keep asking.
Our faces would stop turning to face
the faceless face.

Enough with the hands meeting twice a day.
Enough of expecting change
at the same hour.

If a table bears many weights of items,
the items also depress the upforce
of the table.

The notebook is equally ruined
by the lost wine. The table
is a platform on which to lose.

Surface has no depth but all depth
has this surface. Not on purpose.
So math, not metaphor, works.

I can't charm it open, so charm
is dropped: if't'weren't love,
then love weren't it. Two Ls arranged

as a square keep love outside the frame.
When I came, I was half-coming
You left, half-leaving. A formula.

It's so even-steven, yet so fractal
and Möbius. Yet hagborn. Yet digital.
Calculation is such subtraction,

always figuring what's under
what's under, to break the surface
of the negative realm down

where the wheels don't skid.
Where they may or may not skid.
Where we don't know.

Where we look at signs, like Five of Cups,
a sign of a set of four cups inside
one big cup, which is a drain,

which is why you are weak.
Sourced. Circled protractorlike,
found will be our clock lock,

our night watch, our clear sign.
It's an invisible bend
in the lightsticks, it's a prophecy.

Why Is the Color of Snow?

Let's ask a poet with no way of knowing.
Someone who can give us an answer,
another duplicity to help double the world.

What kind of poetry is all question, anyway?
Each question leads to an iceburn,
a snownova, a single bed spinning in space.

Poet, decide! I am lonely with questions.
What is snow? What isn't?
Do you see how it is for me.

Melt yourself to make yourself more clear
for the next observer.
I could barely see you anyway.

A blizzard I understand better,
the secrets of many revealed as one,
becoming another on my only head.

It's true that snow takes on gold from sunset
and red from rearlights. But that's occasional.
What is constant is white,

or is that only sight, a reflection of eyewhites
and light? Because snow reflects only itself,
self upon self upon self,

is a blanket used for smothering, for sleeping.
For not seeing the naked, flawed body.
Concealing it from the lover curious, ever curious!

Who won't stop looking.
White for privacy.
Millions of privacies to bless us with snow.

Don't we melt it?
Aren't we human dark with sugar hot to melt it?
Anyway, the question—

if a dream is a construction, then what
is not a construction? If a bank of snow
is an obstruction, then what is not a bank of snow?

A winter vault of valuable crystals
convertible for use only by a zen
sun laughing at us.

Oh Materialists! Thinking matter matters.
If we dream of snow, of banks and blankets
to keep our treasure safe forever,

what world is made, that made us that we keep
making and making to replace the dreaming at last.
To stop the terrible dreaming.

Parthenogenesis

It's easy to make more of myself by eating,
and sometimes easy's the thing.

To be double-me, half the trouble
but not lonely.

Making cakes to celebrate any old day.
Eating too much: the emperor of being used.

Nature, mature and feminized,
naturalizes me naturally by creating

the feeling of being a natural woman,
like a sixteen-year-old getting knocked up

again. To solve that problem,
there's the crispness of not eating,

a pane of glass with a bloody-edged
body, that is, having the baby at the prom

undetected and, in a trance of self-preservation,
throwing it away in the girls' room trash.

Buried under paper towels, silent.
Nothing could be better, for the teenager.

For me, starving, that coreless, useful feeling,
is not making myself smaller

but making myself bigger, inside.
It's prince and pauper both, it's starving artist

and good model in one masterpiece.
It rhymes with *marveling* and that's no accident.

Fullness is dullness. Dreaming's too easy.
But sometimes I don't care.

Sometimes I put in just the right amount,
but then I'm the worst kind of patsy, a chump

giving myself over to myself like a criminal
to the law, with nothing to show for it.

No reward, no news, no truth.
It's too sad to be so ordinary every day.

Like some kind of employee.
Being told what to do. Chop off a finger

to plant in fertilizer (that is, in used animal
food), to grow a finger tree.

More fingers for me. Stop saying *finger*.
I'm the one in charge here.

Stop the madness and just eat the mirror.
Put it in sideways or crush it

into a powder. It doesn't hurt and it works.
Mouth full, don't talk.

Nothing to say. I'll be a whole new person.
I'll make her myself. Then we'll walk away.

We'll say to each other how she's changed.
How we wouldn't have recognized us.

Life as Selected Solids

Enchantment's not spells or delusion but dust.
A film. The natural process of ghosting.

There is no magic if it can't stain and absorb itself.
Otherwise, a necessary membrane

is pulled too soon off the world
(the world, not the State, the world,

which is not the State);

the film now delineates as your biggest organ did.
And no one forgets lost skin.

2

Silversmith, Firesmith, Blacksmith.

Toothless, ageless, argument: wherefore
Block Three is blocked.

And we live there so shall we hammer
it out or burn this winter,

or solder pegs to climb over
to our own soft bodies?

To get inside?
To eat to sleep to sleep to leave?

Only one at a time can all three Smiths
participate as a family.

The din of the hammer means ham
for dinner and pegs indicate

leg of lamb. Since when is meaning
so well dealt

and having went so, meant well?
Time is best of all at its job.

So Smith hunger drops hot
on the F'reverolian nomads who belong here,

as members of an elongated body
of us. We, who live in Block Three,

we can't stop living here every day at once.
And it's so important to learn to play

as a team as the side you play
against is inside. At last.

3

Filly, remember how those stones were so warm
we thought they must be alive?

They were eggish and smooth. The life
inside them too even to be life.

But we insisted
on remaining fooled.

Oh Filly, say you remember
because I think I broke them into even warmer stones.

Old Bed

Coil of metal, coin of wood, two-headed
and soft in the middle. This bed has got to go.

This pink, synthetic honey spoiling
the tea of my life, already steeped into a stupor.

Why must everybody sleep
so long, so often, every night all night,

indulgent as disco people in the '70s?
It's like a fad now faded, trendy and cheap.

Sleep: if everyone put a spike
through their heads and wore paper pants

to work I'd be the one to say "No thanks."
I'm not so insecure that I need

to be ridiculous, to dream, to belong
to the smiling group, like anyone.

I don't need a cult of sleep to tell me to die
every night. I don't trust the world

not to come in and steal my stuff every
night. It's this "every night" business

I have issues with. I can't waste another
third of my life drooling, snuffling,

spilling secrets from my honking mouth.
I'm selling the bed.

Sometimes, awake, listening to you talk
in your sleep, the sunrise would steal

in and cover this bed with a thick spread
of orange cheese. It was unreal, awful,

and I was too warm. I'd turn on the bluish
light to cool down. I think I woke you up.

It seemed our legs were tangled but how
tangled could they be, four numb posts

holding our bodies up against the large
dark night of each other? That weight.

I bent myself in two, in this bed. Too late.
I'm tired of it, awake with it. It's dead.

Spring in Space: A Lecture

1. Consider the Possibilities

So much fabric has been worn away
just by wishing it.

Under your costume I'm naked and the pretty
wind for cooling

the south salts me everywhere. Your hands
find me where there is no science,

only precision. I could sleep for days
without a map.

A sample garden in a possible summer never
occurred to me before.

Why should I comprehend it now? It's a lot.
It's only dusk.

This planet spins so it shouldn't be so hot.
You've never felt the sun

on me. And nothing will fall with the exact
weight of itself until you do.

2. Know Your Limits

Our bodies are stunted with scarce infinity;
with our bodies, we hate stars.

Anything endless begins at the end and moves toward less.
This is why stars die without us

knowing. That and the universal shortage of lifeboats,
which we unknowingly recreate,

on earth, at sea, as if it's a mistake each time.
The message is: *there is never enough,*

though we celebrate the hoax of boundlessness.
Celestial bodies, like our own, perish as if they'd scrimped

on light because they had to pay for it,
and no longer could. And froze like so many little match girls.

That's the brutal truth about the heavens.
It's the worst Dickensian squalor at its heart.

Of which there is none. No wisdom either.
People think that to be "wise" is to be old, owlish,

unbearable, or Chinese. Wrong. No need to wait or be reborn.
To be wise is simply to be understood, even missed.

3. Use Your Imagination

Don't be fooled. It is very easy
to feel nostalgia for the natural
world. As if the cheerily if

ambivalently named month of "May"
"feels" warmth after a sullen
period of icy withholding.

"Forgives." Or that the very earth
"expresses" a gratitude or
tenderness in return for nothing!

Fish don't have feelings. Clouds
are not angry. Spring buds are lucky
accidents, not faith. *Spring* itself is a word

that means a season, a kind of freshwater
and an aerial action. It is, in short,
and within reason, anything we want it to be.

If I had my way, spring would
revolve slowly and solely around me.
Each morning, I'm the earth's

favorite daughter, extremely eating
a breakfast of yolky sun,
a relentless placebo I enjoy alone,

while the rest of the foolish world
suffers continual, half-dead night.
I waited for you for months.

You said, "Spring," and I kept the bed warm,
held a candle. It's way past that now.
Now try to find me in the dark.

Three Summers Mark Only Two Years

No wonder time is so mistaken.

Three summers like any other three summers:

aren't they long and dayful

with traintrips to the sea edge

and free legs? Why do we only get two

years in exchange for three summers?

A full year stolen by mosquitoes.

Like a club sandwich, we need an extra

summer to separate year of bacon

from year of turkey. Like a lot of hard

work taxed a full third. I'll gladly

suffer in a stolen year, make it a year

of sweaty nights alone in a cube

and days in a cubicle,

time spent to buy time. I'll take

a year of that. Just give it back to me.

One Love Story, Eight Takes

Where you are tender, you speak your plural.
Roland Barthes

I

One version of the story is I wish you back—
that I used each evening evening out
what all day spent wrinkling.

I bought a dress that was so extravagantly feminine
you could see my ovaries through it.

This is how I thought I would seduce you.
This is how frantic I hollowed out.

2

Another way of telling it
is to hire some kind of gnarled

and symbolic troll to make
a tape recording.

Of plastic beads coming unglued
from a child's jewelry box.

This might be an important sound,
like serotonin or mighty mitochondria,

so your body hears about
how you stole the ring made

from a glittery opiate
and the locket that held candy.

3

It's only fair that I present yet another side,
as insidious as it is,

because two sides hold up nothing but each other.

A tentacled skepticism,
a suspended contempt,

such fancies and toxins form a third wall.

A mean way to end
and I never dreamed we meant it.

4

Another way of putting it is like
slathering jam on a scrape.

Do sweets soothe pain or simply make it stick?
Which is the worst! So much technology
and no fix for sticky if you can't taste it.

I mean there's no relief unless.
So I'm coming, all this excitement,

to your house. To a place where there's no room for play.
It is possible you'll lock me out and I'll finally
focus on making mudcakes look solid in the rain.

5

In some cultures the story told is slightly different—
in that it is set in an aquarium and the audience participates

as various fish. The twist comes when it is revealed
that the most personally attractive fish have eyes

only on one side and repel each other like magnets.
The starfish is the size of an eraser and does as much damage.

Starfish, the eponymous and still unlikely hero, has
those five pink moving suckerpads

that allow endless permutations so no solid memory,
no recent history, nothing better, left unsaid.

6

The story exists even when there are no witnesses,
kissers, tellers. Because secrets secrete,

and these versions tend to be slapstick, as if in a candy
factory the chocolate belted down the conveyor too fast

or everyone turned sideways at the same time by accident.
This little tale tries so hard to be humorous,

wants so badly to win affection and to lodge.
Because nothing is truly forgotten *and* loved.

7

Three million Richards can't be wrong.
So when they levy a critique of an undertaking which,

in their view, overtakes, I take it seriously.
They think one may start a tale off whingy

and wretched in a regular voice.
But when one strikes out whimsically,

as if meta-is-betta, as if *it isn't you,*
as if this story is *happening to nobody*

it is only who you are fooling that's nobody.
The Richards believe you cannot

privately jettison into the sky, just for fun.
You must stack stories from the foundation up.

From the sad heart and the feet tired of supporting it.
Language is architecture, after all, not an air capsule,

not a hang glide. This is real life.
So don't invite anyone to a house that hasn't been built.

Because no one unbuilds meticulously
and meticulosity is what allows hearing.

Three million Richards make one point.
I hear it in order to make others. Mistakes.

8

As it turns out, there is a wrong way to tell this story.
I was wrong to tell you how multi-true everything is,

when it would be truer to say nothing.
I've invented so much and prevented more.

But, I'd like to talk with you about other things,
in absolute quiet. In extreme context.

To see you again, isn't love revision?
It could have gone so many ways.

This just one of the ways it went.
Tell me another.

AMBROSIA

I'm Perfect at Feelings,

so I have no problem telling you
why you cried over the third lost
metal or the mousetrap. I knew
that orgasms weren't your fault
and that feeling of keeping solid
in yourself but wanting an ecstatic
black hole was just bad beauty.

Certain loves were perfect
in the daytime and had every
right to express carnally behind
the copy machine and there are
no hard feelings for the boozy
sodomy and sorry XX daisy chain,
whenever it felt right for you.

And when the moment of soft
levitation with erasing hands
made you feel dirty, like
the main person to think up love
in the first place, I knew that.
It's okay, you're an innocent
with the brilliance of an animal

stuffing yourself sick on a kill.
Don't, don't feel like the runt alien
on my ship: I get you. I know
the dimensions of your wishing
and losing and don't think you
a glutton with petty beefs. But
even I, who know your triggers,

your emblematic sacs of sad fury,
I understand why the farthest fat trees

sliver down with your disappointment
and why the big sense of the world,
wrong before you, shrugs but
somewhere grasps your spinning,
stunning, alone. But you have me.

Breasted Landscape

If not so cloaked with the desire
to be the ravishing little transparency,
I'd have seen the autumn for what
it is: just scrambled math and nipples.

The occasional warm hand sandwich.
Red leaves are bendy scabs of wine,
married to the ground and still looking.
Parasites flinging their own bodies to keep

others' clean. I'd linger further
with you over yellow fat and never
be that berry-stained girl we take
turns being.

But now huge on the bed, the sheet
one quivery flake of baklava,
your sleep beats me utterly underneath.
There is no light under the moss

under us. Your feet are the most
curiously square cathedral
whores science can prove, taking you
from me, with exquisite archery

to the next curve, hysterical exile.
Can't have you there.
Where trees knot up permanently
at each of their stomachaches

and if cried at, won't listen,
not exploding with the human gas
of losing-again, that blown-glass liquid.
A side-feeling rips me, everything

is you. Hello, belly smell, where's
the steriler air?
I've lost you in the choking dark,
but I brought you there.

Sorry, T.

but I'm a ghost. Do you understand
that the person you love
is fleshy and heavy from hip

to boot to make up for this?
There's a name for it: Brenda,
but I can't fool everyone.

Even if I have convinced you,
and I don't bruise easily, that I am yours
to strong-arm and throttle.

Even when you force me to become
of this world—of this cold floor:
I can do so only for a moment.

When the moment falls off
and primal fool-seasons
affix their wintry incubus,

I tend to stomp around to another
bed. Hurting you vaporizes me,
which is why I love others.

I don't leave a flukeprint in the sweat
of things. The ground won't greet me
like a domestic animal when I walk.

When I talk you glaze over like the sun
on shifty pavement.
I won't see the lip of a step

before I bloody my knees again.
(The blood isn't so bad, but for a ghost
it doesn't make sense.

Others can draw it, they don't know.
They make it into a potion for themselves
but you try to make me look at it.)

Drift

I'll go anywhere to leave you but come with me.
All the cities are like you anyway. Windows
darken when I get close enough to see.
Any place we want to stay's polluted,

the good spots taken already by those
who ruin them. And restaurants we'd never find.
We'd rut a ditch by a river in nights
so long they must be cut by the many pairs

of wrong-handled scissors maybe god owns
and doesn't share. I water god.
I make a haunted lake and rinse and rinse.
I take what I want, and have ever since what

I want disappeared, like anything hunted.
That's what you said. Disappointment
isn't tender, dried and wide instead.
The tourists snapped you crying,

and the blanket I brought was so dirty
it must have been lying around
in lice and blood that whole year we fought.
It wasn't clear, so I forgot.

I haven't been sleeping, next to you
twitching to bury my boring eyes.
The ship made you sad, and the ferry, and canoe.
All boats do.

Three Sorries

1. I'm Sorry

I hid your life vest in the death trap on purpose, my love.
I'd hoped you'd die, and in this way, live. Sorry.

Three snakes asked me three questions each,
each requiring three answers.

My answers, thrice tripled,
looped back around to the natural sounds

of just forgetting, of the tenderly adjusted.

Soon   (1) Born: 1970
               (2) Cried: all along
               (3) Loved: you really so very much and no others

blurred into: (1) begging off for the dog-years behavior
                    (2) extra heart hidden in sock drawer
                    (3) undetected slept with others

It's not as if, it wasn't because, I didn't mean
it three to the thirtieth power and replacement.

All seemed collapsible into one sentence,
which I hope you can read into: I'm sorry.

2. Don't Be Sorry

Keep doing it!
Make the red lead ball float on the black
snow of a small man's monstrous land.

The details distract me from the basic landscape.
Lurid with everyone young,
all singing toward a patch of backbends

and no pain, your lavender plane aims
for a wet landing
between two pointed green breasts.

And, drunk, just makes it.
Will do it again this way, calm as a skunk
on the road, smelling cars and so certain

that cars smell her. But they don't.
Throw your body over the many-storied ledge
again, to prove you can't undo it.
And further, wouldn't. Won't.

3. How Can I Not Be?

You make me sound so bad. At our miserable dinner,
even my own chewing disgusted me, as if I'd borrowed
myself from you, with a weak smile. *I promise I'll give it back.*

Stories with no sex, no terse, conspicuous absence
of sex and no characters you can project sex onto
never get picked out to read in bed,

nervous about, but hoping for, sex.
You're a big, crazy skeleton with black, mean hair
and the same eyes. Same stalky hands fluid as always

carving into the same groove so as to seem endless
but there's no surprise, just that pinch of you moving
like mercury to look as unfathomable as time or trash.

Tell me a new story, one you don't know the middle of.
There's only so much I can take, that's the mistake.
And I take it back, I'm not sorry. Not sorry at all.

Replaceable until You're Not.

Throw your love until it sticks, and know
        you'll only know it stuck

if it ends up sticking. In case it does
        in the end, in the beginning

just say "This is the one." Whether or not
        that's true, trick yourself

into it being true, so you're someone
        who says truths.

The problem might be regret. It is so beautiful
        to cry and remember,

if beauty is a knife wound. Memory, that disco light,
        makes for some unforgettable songs,

until morning. *Will I have you?* It's impossible
        to know, or impossible to have a person.

Why do we think we can?
        I can't yet forget the quiet music you gave me,

the lyrics I imagined in your voice.
        Music's ruthless that way: "Here are the words

and here's the tune to how you feel. Doesn't matter
        you didn't originate your own feelings.

We know you! Enjoy!" I may be a chump,
        but at some point aren't I irreplaceable?

And if I am, mustn't I have always been,
       or have I so improved?

2

When does being enough occur? When will I say
       you and no other, you as long

as I can see, as long as I want, and I want infinitely.
       Not indefinitely, which seems arbitrary,

but wanting precisely more, always,
       of the same kind of thing.

When, because next year never happens, the wedding
       plans sketched on scraps of paper

thrown out next misunderstanding. Fresh pages
       replace them. Fresh scraps.

Eventually the heart I have to offer
       is as hard and small and uni-purpose as a tack.

3

We only make this love work because we work for it,
       like a wage, an art.

We are only each other's because
       the day is long.

The feeling, the opening wide, the blue glee,
       laughing, ravenous together.

And at some point the question comes up,
       of whether we could continue

and the answer is not quite yes, which isn't quite no,
        but then what is it?

Well, we both deserve something more than nothing,
        neither of which this thing we're doing ends up being.

So let's split, let's know, and make ourselves an old song of it:
        "If I'm not it then it's not me and you neither."

Moving on, is what they call it. As if one moves,
        instead of revises, reneges, replenishes.

When you get new shoes, do you throw out the old?
        Do you buy the same style?

4

Not another one, you think, impossible.
        Not again.

I can't do it differently, I can't do it
        the same. I can't.

You do. Opening. Being careful.
        Being stupid.

Same beast of hope, beast of shame,
        same terror, same space, different world.

Old world. Scary moment. Amazement
        that breaks you.

You are not broken. You break again
        and again because

that's what breaking means.
        To be whole.

5

Maybe when we're in the same nursing home,
        neighbors again after decades apart,

surprised at our homing instinct. Or maybe just
        next year, happy with others,

having learned not to chuck the safe before cracking it.
        At a friend's book party,

you'll notice how I've changed. In line
        at the Apple Store, weary in the cab,

startled in the saladmarket, weepy at the doctor's,
        I'll never change.

6

I'll always be the same woman you loved,
        this woman I no longer am,

I'll be her and re-be her
        because I can't replace myself.

Hers is the body you loved, she was yours,
        this future corpse;

no matter how many lovers she, her body, and I have,
        only you know the curvature that stops your heart,

that's the truth of it, only you could hear
        the mess of breaths and cries I make splitting open,

my voice cracking in your arms
        even when this corpse is a corpse.

Because it all happened to me, the real actual me.
        I am yours. I am still I.

You must be still part-me, but who wasn't,
        parting ways. You could always replace me,

go ahead, find another to fill the me-shaped hole.
        I would do the same.

Find a new person I'd also call *you*,
        another I'd hold with my cold, dead hands.

You Too, Not Just Me

Never just me.
However you need,

however, I'll be.
Like smoke slid

in like previous whiskey,
fire wisps,

fire drowns.
And follows itself

into new form,
first

afraid it's too alike.
A fraud must

believe, too.
Then, forgetting

how unlikely.
A centaur's first street

fair, alone.
Then so lucky,

only a dream is so lucky.
Sometimes laughing

with others
who must sense

us, condensed,
frontbodied, pushing

soft walking
circles onto a ledge.

Imperceptible
where your face

turns into breath
and vanishes

in the home.
Can't matter

in the home.
Some fire

makes form
only folly,

however all three
follow us to take

your shape
down with mine.

Straight's the New Gay

Because if you are a woman you should fall for another
at least once in your life

unless you are in that deviant minority of women
claiming to be 110 percent heterosexual.

In that case it is an imperative: defy your nature.
Get rid of that too-protesty 10 percent.

You, more so than normal women, will fall harder
than you ever imagined.

Your bruises will be museum-quality Ming Dynasty
frog-blossoms uprooting your veins.

Words like *penis-substitute* or *lifestyle*,
as applied to yours,

will wound and incite you into daily little wars.
This is a regime change.

Nevertheless, still a regime. You will be gayer
than the most-aborted genes,

more lesbian than anything else you will ever be.
In this way you are erased

(you've known it and feared it all along) from science,
discourse, your careers.

This is how we do it to you: we keep you extremes
to either side

and parade down the middle while you cheer us on.

Vagile

It's not so bad, this imaginary math,
this halving and doubling.
Is half of nothing a double-not?

No one asked. No one heard
fire hit the mirror
before it turned black.

So no one got
an equation that seemed inexact.
I did nothing with love,

let it use me as feet use a body's weight.
Jumping rope, jumping ship.
I am senseless in the water, but loud,

and your slim body is coming
through the blind spot even I can see.
Coming in silence as I listen too hard.

Straining for the sound
of your helplessness to me.
My own voice calling you to lie

here on *this* plank, has to be *this* one
and no other, where it echoes
and we're inside everything.

Once, the melting made clear
our godbaby and I was never alone.
But you were. Young,

no closer to me than a little boy
looking up at an airplane.
It made me crazy. I was you!

And you are not so young.
Make noise. Be my animal
so I know my body is a home.

How can I be a woman?
How can I be only this half?

This Loved Body

The skin moving over your rib cage is like liquid lead rubbing over a gravestone, but how could you resemble stone, poison? Am I so certain my proofs of love won't stop you cold? Now you breathe, now still.

2

The shoulder curves in Möbius. Where convex collapses concave it is without formality, only form. Without agreeing to, one camel lies down to become a kitten, fine-whiskered, its throat pulsing tinily on the skyborne Tokyo expressway, as long and as quick.

3

This belly is hardly what I call a belly. Could there be less belly in it? I am accustomed to women's bellies, of which there is usually some. You seem like a machine here, hairless and olive. But when you bend you are as human as can be, literally within an inch of your life. Because the machinery is in plain view; you have no secret stash, nothing for winter, nothing to lose. In an emergency, this would be an emergency. I am horrified, my thinlet, and won't ever let you be hungry.

4

Between navel and genitals there is almost nothing, hairwise. Free forgotten parking space. Like you gave yourself a break. Until the work suddenly begins in a dark bloom, so localized, as carefully plotted as an English garden. These hairs are the dark, curved lines that stars traveled toward their brightness. These hairs are mother bears, protective. There are cosmic and natural laws about them. They have properties.

5

The weight and delicate gravity of your genitals makes me suffer. Your exposure, your aging, your difference. The way your *seiki* pulls down the skin, inner pelvis, is unassailable, so certain of how things are. As fine as the nascent laxities under your jaw in your thirty-third year. As lovely as folded silk for a daughter someday.

6

The fingers of one hand can open a cellophane-wrapped box of condoms, pull one out, rid the circle of its square and unroll the new cylinder onto yourself. While the other hand picks a guitar. The index and middle fingers can cut like beautiful scissors. The thumbs are weapons on the soles of my feet. These hands absorb the fire licking down the arms, blue and green and amber, but the only trace of a burn is a shiny wedge scar from a street fight that these hands may or may not have started.

7

I watched you in the bath from a certain angle. *Seiki* tucked underneath, thighs in a smooth pout, long black hair threatening the surface of the water. And an illusion making your far hip swell, this angle narrowing your shoulder, the line of your jaw sharp and soft. All your calves, ankles, and feet as tightly curved as in archery and aimed at me somehow. Calves frugally downed and heavy, a woman's. Feet as in wide, high heels. A man. Toes balanced as if on top of a weather vane. And your knees as vulnerable as lemonpeel smelling of nothing.

That's not an ass, I thought when I first saw it, extra naked as if nearly sans itself. Only the blueprints of an ass. Later the ass seemed to grow flesh in the dark, latent musculature and roundness filled my hands where my eyes could see nothing. An imaginary fruit disappearing out of season.

9

I return to these legs because of breathlessness, which is what beauty uses to deny me the luxury of description. I can only examine. The leg hairs worn off by the daily rubbing of jeans and boots, thus achieving naturally a girlish smoothness, whereas I slice myself daily for a gravelly facsimile of this surface. This calf could not be more lavishly flared without bursting, already as wide around as a thigh and tapered to a sinewed virgin ankle. Made of birdbones and fetus skull.

The thigh is long and it never relaxes, like an ogre's magic flute. The flat, turgid muscle running the outside laps can hardly be touched, mesmerized by its lifetime role as stoic, mover, and outsider.

What about this body makes it Japanese? The hair and its hairlessness, the goldish skin, thinness, essentially? The curves so modest as to be mistaken for straight lines and the many straight lines, as if the body kept itself in line all its life.

In Kabuki performance, the actor momentously strikes a pose called a *mie*—a human signature and expert timing collaborating with the staccato beat of the *tsuke*, the wooden clappers announcing the coming *mie*. Suspense is tight and high as the actor's body stretches out infinitely, arm and hand extended indefinitely. The *tsuke* are wild with communication, and at last: the hand flares, the eyes cross demonically, the head wobbles as if reeling from the immense weight of its own insight. What everyone realizes now is that something has really happened.

13

Naked and alone with me this body moves in a sequence of *mie*, heralded by *tsuke* I am too Western to hear or time. When you hit your natural pose it is a surprise, dramatic arm, hand flexed, eyes fierce. Legs holding both up and down the exact weight of you and nothing more. I can't claim to understand this art. But I understand it is art by the pleasure I take in it. In its uselessness. This beauty is relentless, even as you retract, unperturbed, fully inhabiting. But what art do I have to repeat you senseless?

14

The hair is wiry, thick on the head. About two feet long, its curl is pulled down by its length to a slight wave hello. There are two copper streaks because, in Tokyo, everyone has given themselves some form of gold treatment. Experimental relief from everybody else. Fear of the automatic nature of nature.

15

Above the eyes you have symmetrical awnings so perfected as to be overlooked, except in rain. The eyelashes peek out and up, two or three roots joined at the tip to make a starfringe on how you see.

16

The voice, is it a part of the body?

Your mouth is full and rosy, lined with a kind of brown stain that matches you behind the ears. The lower lip is almost spherical. It was the first thing I noticed about you. It lowers your face to eye level and this is the language I know in circles. This mouth, however, speaks Japanese, the designation of this mind. My language is a glutinate gumming up the works of this mouth, which, when it is free to speak its natural mind, is awash. I am so gloriously dumb. I wish I knew what you were saying.

17

I wish you were saying it to me. All I glean is the music and your involvement in it, your mind at work taking it easy. You sound like a simmering stew. I sound like an espresso machine. The mouth soothes and translates, wakes and translates, so occupied it is empty with translation.

18

Small eyes are misunderstood. They have survived the invasion of the face not without cost. And not without a constituent mercy. The deep mercy of staying still without hiding. Of being themselves without being "like." Resembling other eyes, magnified, hypnotized. Yours are disparate, asymmetrical. One eye is always closer to sleep, the other, more practical. Both with a stark, glinted color I've never seen anywhere but in there. But what is seeing?

19

What is a lover's body? This one is covered with a substance I know to be skin but feels more like a bird's egg lightly brushed with rain oil. Somewhere underneath is a shower of garnets which sometimes graze the skin's film, electrical alizarin diffracted through the finest scrim.

20

And gold, of course. What is skin if not, in some aspect, gold? Some parts of this body actually glitter with it. These are the softest parts. So soft I suspect they were meant to be inside and kept secret.

Me in Paradise

Oh, to be ready for it, unfucked, ever-fucked.
To have only one critical eye that never
divides a flaw from its lesson.

To play without shame. To be a woman
who feels only the pleasure of being used
and who reanimates the user's

anguished release in a land
for the future to relish, to buy
new tights for, to parade in fishboats.

To scare up hope without fear of hope,
not holding the hole, I will catch
the superbullet in my throat

and feel its astounding force
with admiration. Absorbing its kind
of glory. I must be someone

with very short arms to have lost you,
to be checking the windows
of the pawnshop renting space in my head,

which pounds with all the clarity
of a policeman on my southernmost door.
To wish and not jinx it: to wish

and not fish for it: to wish and forget it.
To ratchet myself up with hot liquid
and find a true surprise.

Prowling the living room for the lightning,
just one more shock,
to bring my slow purity back.

To miss you without being so damn cold
all the time. To hold you without dying otherwise.
To die without losing death as an alternative.

To explode with flesh, without collapse.
To feel sick in my skeleton, in all the serious
confetti of my cells, and know why.

Loving you has made me so scandalously
beautiful. To give myself to everyone but you.
To luck out of you. To make any other mistake.

ASTROLABE

Embarrassment

It's a wave, isn't it? Not a particle.
A fresh, cool wave, so why am I flushed
and not washed?
Why dirtier than before?

1. Etymology

On the subject of our names.
They're so embracing,
thinking they're all us

and swallowing themselves
into our nausea.

Yet we never quite die on the spot.
We put off being what we're called,
we take the hint.

Time is never wasted.
It is always spent.

2. Teleology

Sheer fabric trailing through 4 a.m.
I thought it was opaque and earlier.

3. Mathematics

I know you know I know.
And the mirror multiplies inside.

The world is no bigger, but next time
do the math,

because I wanted to know none
of what I now know twice.

4.The Principle of the Borg

Saying "There's no one like me"
accomplishes the exact opposite
of what you mean.

It is true only insofar as it is true
for everyone equally.

So it means you are not special
in any way. Which should be enough for you.

5. Documentary

This clothing, a maladaptive wrapping,
cuts me up. I am a vignette,

floated knowingly
since I pulled myself through myself,

like a unitard. Too many eyeholes

have been cut and pieced together
to make flesh less various with others.

6. Medicine

The cure for embarrassment
is substitution.

Strap, don't pluck.
Baldness makes headlines.

Use grass. Use less.
Shorts under your skirt for recess.

Redo the surfaces of your wrong turns to make
taking them smoother in the future.

7. Cosmology

Things are less embarrassing
at the cellular level. Remember?

We were a whole part of the universe
before Mother busted the party.

Before we were ourselves.
Now, like dirty soap, we

attract what we repel.

8. Apology

Even the clumsiest fate is perfectly shaped,
so the view took over looking

but the sweetest thing I've ever known
is obscene with a beautiful

sugar rotted down to its truth.

Loving you a serious accidental shame
and day flatulates into night,

trips and falls in front of millions
into morning.

In thrall to this pocus:
the end of fear starts

with such an annihilating blush,
with such a stutter.

A Poet's Poem

If it takes me all day,
I will get the word *freshened* out of this poem.

I put it in the first line, then moved it to the second,
and now it won't come out.

It's stuck. I'm so frustrated,
so I went out to my little porch all covered in snow

and watched the icicles drip, as I smoked
a cigarette.

Finally I reached up and broke a big, clear spike
off the roof with my bare hand.

And used it to write a word in the snow.
I wrote the word *snow*.

I can't stand myself.

First Date and Still Very, Very Lonely

A pleasant, leather poison
is the trick to smelling
good to female saddles,

that is, saddles with a hole
and not a pommel. Remember
those? Gone the way

of vestal virgins and tight,
white black holy hell and with it,
the lesbian Elysium of old.

I miss the idea of wives.
The loving circle.
But onward. Today

is a sacred day. A date day.
An exception to the usual
poor me, poor me!

I'm not poor and I'm not me.
I remember both
states as soon ago as last week.

But that's history.
This is different. At a party,
once, everyone was so careful

that only I cut my lip drinking
from the winterspring,
a kind of cold, decorative trough

centerpiece we were all
drinking from. The idea is
you're like animals.

If you ask, about the cut, *Why me?*
The answer is, *Of course me.*
In what world ever possible not *me?*

I could admit that with open blood
running down my chin
like hyena butter or gasoline.

I was mortified, really lost.
After that I thought,
I have to meet someone.

No Such Thing as One Bee

Do I look like a bee?
One cell of a hiveswarm
individually striped.

Using winter as a way
to act as an egg
among many, a potential

sameness. Using spring
to syringe mass progeny
into the tiny sexes

everywhere deskirted.
Do I look so capable of the tasks
embedded in my bee-

body? Not distracted by
a nice voice. Not even having
to try, bumbling

from home to queen
to bare summer leg to
a cellular death

more drowse than death.
Each year more of me, each
year new rumors

I'm a killer this time. Not
just a seasonal martyr
for the queen

but some group intelligence
sharpening to a point.
Do I look so sophisticated

that I could be a bee,
that I could choose to hurt you,
and it would not be my choice?

Moth Death on the Windowsill

1. Moth's Last Words to You

Being sexy is so important to humans, it's repulsive
but what's not to love? The way you pay in warm
soft cash, erasing cigarettes so coolly. Plus you're so big.

I warned you people, never sleep with the one you love.
Sleep with the others. Make 'em want you,
and you'll love 'em soon enough. Just use the body.

And as for women, for those who love women,
please remember you can always get back inside.
You really can, pressing the emptiness on your hands

and knees. Involve her when your best ideas come,
i.e., Wallace Stevens was addicted to candy, a great
idea for a movie to make together: women love this.

2. My Last Words to You

Let's get a little digital camera and one of those film-
making programs and finally do this thing.
Let's become an art team and make a family of films.

We're a messy couple, admit it, and what we put
on-screen could delight us, relight us with proof
of us, memory-proof! Forget Stevens, here's the subject:

The moth died in a minisecond falling the half-inch
between the window and the screen. If such a little
makes a difference then a little is a lot.

Unless a dying is not. The moth is nothing,
but a whole death? More than we've managed
to accomplish at this window. We waited

for our software to be delivered,
we barely watched. We missed it, missed
the window. Missed our shot.

Don't Be So Small, Poet

is something you might say.
Don't be only that small.

If you can't be big, at least
be premolecular, viral, microbial,

be a poet of existence,
go smaller and more

insinuating, in eachness.
No one needs an everyday poet.

We have desks and their visible
dust. We don't need more

of that to clean.
Five pieces of wood turned

into an inch of ash in an hour.
Who wants to know?

We need a poet of the nanosecond
and of the subparticle

because the dimensions have no hair-
line cracks that I can see.

Who can slip between them?
The fire I made in the firebox

preceded the ash it became.
Preceded it with wood

and wood-knots with hairs
that caught flame mixed

with air. Which part are you
now part of?

Nothing is you now. But
breaths and rays and waves

and inklings *of what* are you
coming through on?

Where are you going
if not to more of yourself?

When your lover left, no one
could find you except

in hurt rage. Now you've
left and I still can't find you.

I can hurt. I can rage.
I was never your lover.

But why didn't you ever write me back?
You were always writing.

Perhaps a letter wasn't big enough.
Some poet needs to get

so small she can skitter
like a bead of water on a hot pan,

and slip into the world between worlds,
and find out where you went,

Susan. Someone small enough
to touch your hand in a taxicab

and get back out with news
of the next big thing you're writing.

(for Susan Sontag 1933–2004)

Dancing in My Room Alone

I could be an eel in whirled stillwaters,
the semiotic blue of trick quicksand,
meaningless and true.

In my room, ordinary yellow objects
like lapel labels and plates
smile like similes,

caressed like air in movies,
the texture of froth. I need sugar.
Need it like a right, so sugar

is given. A river of high
minutes rising to a horizon,
only ever seeing my double eyes.

I'm so really truly enough
that I should save myself for later.
Later, don't come now.

Don't turn me back into that seventh-
grader in a human ring around the gym,
certain I'm not in the circle.

Now I'm slinging room-darkness
to sun. Swelling hips
incredibly undone,

my blind blood singing,
"qua aqua aqua,"
intoxicated

with this song's cologne,
a silk ribbon of paint
driven through nature.

Fun, who knew? Spinning
with nothing, as earth does,
I flew more than I could lose.

O god of ether, god of vapor,
I could use one of either of you.
Take me as a swan would.

Take me, wing me up and make me
dance, impaled on a hooked
prick of cyclone.

Sightless. Wind my limbs, digits
clutching feathers, around you,
and disappear.

I won't fall. I know how to do it now.
I broke the window with god's ball.
I am smoothly used

and honeyed, self-twinned, fearless,
a wineskin emptying
into a singing stranger.

Fathometer

Detected by simple vibration,
there is only one source

for the infinite plugs.
Love is the source, of course,

the exposed wire in water
still working. The exception.

We know this because all
other sources deplete.

In depths the signals signal,
O universal code, note how

the Milky Way registers
its dustiest guest.

All symbols match their
incarnates as if practically,

no matter what key is used
to open the throat. How dark

the hole. How the wind floats.
Here is the coat that covers

the body that exposes a winter
mindful of spring

under the bed for later.
But now on the bed is the body.

Sleeping through the party.
And under the body, a pile

of coats. A balance
no matter what the weight is.

Once a month
the next month comes.

Once a month the boat is broken
because the moon is not.

It means, stay home, human,
if you're leaking. Or does it mean,

there is nothing you need
unsubmerged. So speak.

So poor in our weather we strike
a match that the wind knows

better than to snuff. We steal
and peak and have enough.

Magician

You woke up crying,
"Why did our baby die?"

I said, "You're dreaming.
We don't have a baby."

"Yes we do. But it died."
You're sobbing, sweaty.

"Look, sweetheart, you said 'it.'
That proves we don't have a baby.

If we had one, you would say 'she'
or 'he.'" I smooth your hair.

I kiss your cheek. Your temperature
has cooled. You're asleep again.

It would have a name.
"His name or her name

always disappears just before
I wake up."

And also just before you fall asleep.
Nothing ever really happens.

A Brown Age

Summer took every one of my
dresses while I was having
them perfumed;

summer wore them every day
so I was naked and living in a cave
where frugivores

snuffled in the melonflesh.
I wrote you a letter in dirty ink.
Asking you here.

Why not? Trees move
at least as much as we do,
if only their heads and arms.

I didn't write that.
I scratched it
on a rock and skipped the rock.

Brownie, the pink oranges are hanging
just behind your head.
It's the life you can't see.

If I turned your head, you'd still
only see the turning.
Not fruit. Not me.

But legs moved to prove you came
at all. At last, we were sleeping
and fucking and it was fall.

Now in the dark brown dark,
it's cold and white.
Your eyes are largely

plural like fish
sleepfloating in their zones,
no souls, but thirsty.

On the mouth of the cave,
there is an icicle that had no way
here in summer.

Now it melts down
and refreezes into the shape
of a wishbone or two wet

legs to escape on. I will break
them both and put it all in a cup.
I'll wish for water,

that is, waste a wish on what
will already come.
Please don't leave.

Please drink it. I'm waiting
for noon to become midnight
and for you to drink it.

ABOUT THE AUTHOR

Brenda Shaughnessy is the author of *Interior with Sudden Joy*.
Her poems have been published in *Bomb, Conjunctions, McSweeney's, The New Yorker, The Paris Review,* and elsewhere. She is the poetry editor of *Tin House* magazine and has taught poetry at many institutions, including Eugene Lang College and Princeton University. She lives in Brooklyn with her husband and son.

The Chinese character for poetry is made up of two parts: "word" and "temple." It also serves as pressmark for Copper Canyon Press.

Since 1972, Copper Canyon Press has fostered the work of emerging, established, and world-renowned poets for an expanding audience. The Press thrives with the generous patronage of readers, writers, booksellers, librarians, teachers, students, and funders—everyone who shares the belief that poetry is vital to language and living.

Major funding has been provided by:
Anonymous (2)
Beroz Ferrell & The Point, LLC
Lannan Foundation
National Endowment for the Arts
Cynthia Lovelace Sears and Frank Buxton
Washington State Arts Commission

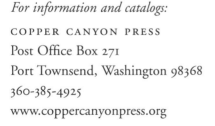

For information and catalogs:
COPPER CANYON PRESS
Post Office Box 271
Port Townsend, Washington 98368
360-385-4925
www.coppercanyonpress.org

The typeface is Janson, designed by Hungarian traveling scholar Nicholas Kis in the 1680s. Display type is Gill Sans, a humanist sans serif typeface designed by Eric Gill between 1927 and 1930. Gill was a well-established sculptor, graphic artist, and type designer. The Gill Sans typeface takes inspiration from Edward Johnston's Johnston typeface for the London Underground, which Gill had worked on while apprenticed to Johnston. Book design and composition by Phil Kovacevich. Printed on archival-quality Glatfelter Author's Text at McNaughton & Gunn, Inc.